I'm Not Your Laughing Daughter

Ellen Bass

I'm not your laughing daughter

The University of Massachusetts Press Amherst 1973

Contents

Crying among the cases of Cliquot Club and pints of Tiger Rose

I am in the back room of our liquor store
crying among the cases of Cliquot Club
            and pints of Tiger Rose
looking at the floor where boards close the stairs
            at my face in the peeling mirror above the
                        yellow sink and yellow soap.

My grandmother is lying on a couch
saying tomorrow
        when she's stronger
        she'll put on her rings.

My father is in the front of the store
                waiting on a customer
                asking fifths or quarts.
My father says she should be in a home
                until she's finished dying.

Pleasantville, New Jersey

When I was a child, I hated the rabbi whose saliva formed a rubber
                    band between his lips
and loved Eddie Stecher in the jewelry store a block up Main Street.
I wished my watch said Stecher on it like the clock outside his store
                    instead of Whittnauer.
I had a long-torso dress, a red and green print with tick tack toes,
          a charcoal sweater set,
              and, through the years, dozens of those stretchy puckered tube tops.

On Sundays, I'd walk my bike to the Acme parking lot with my mother.
She'd hold the seat while I peddled,
                          circling the lot like a circus pony.
One time I really got going, balancing steady,
              mother running along till I rode on my own,
              peddling and peddling,
              heading for the concrete boulder.
I screamed and peddled faster.

There were caterpillars in the spring, caterpillars
crawling all over the dirt road between my house and Pat and Nancy's,
          behind the oily garage
          behind the electric company and the lady-with-the-lilacs' house.
I hated them.
I could take one caterpillar. One with no others around,
          sitting quietly, or, if moving, moving in front of me.
I could watch one that way.
That way I could probably even touch one,
          put my finger on its back, feel the fuzzy bristles.
But there were millions of them, around my feet
                              hanging from Pat and Nancy's fingers,
                              ready to jump on my neck
                                  or down my back,
                              without me even knowing.

We played serious games when I was a child.
Not games really, but plays,

               making it up as we went along,
               often a love story, or with someone dying.
I'd lean over Nancy in the bed,
      delivering my lines,
and I was that person.
I wasn't trying to recall that night when Uncle Ben dropped dead:
      how did I feel?
      Recapture that and play it for the audience.
There was no audience
              and I'd slept through his heart attack.
I was this mourner.

There were other plays we'd do:
                  The King and the Slave Girl.
I sat on Pat's lap, forced there by the castle guards (that's Nancy)
      who found me in the royal woods.
Pat would lift my t-shirt and fondle my flat breasts.
We never reversed roles.
I couldn't be the king, didn't know what to do.
But I could play that slave girl.

One time Pat dared us to sit naked in my bathtub until she counted 100.
      I think she didn't know how to count
      because she did it silently.
We waited, sitting in the cold tub,
      until, after a while,
      it must have been longer than 100,
I heard my mother coming up the stairs, opening the door:
      "Girls, don't sit around catching cold."

Once after Pat and Nancy moved to Northfield, I went to visit them
      and we played Doctor in the woods,

5

curing ourselves by chewing leaves
                    or rubbing sap on our hands.
For the worst disease, we pulled down our pants
                    and put smooth stones between our lips,
                feeling the cold of the dry stone
                            between our warmth.

I can remember it was July
and we had spaghetti that night
before I went home.

Did you ever say I love you?

I. to my father

She says you used to sing and
I remember it, riding in the car,
mother and I in the back,
you and Herb in the front.
I'd lean over the seat
while you sang, "A carpet of roses I'd
lay at your feet, for you, for you."
Was that really you?

She says when you were courting,
she liked to hear you whistle,
walking down the street whistling.
What did it look like, I wonder?
Was it summer? and were there
cars parked at the curb?
Did it smell of cabbage and
was the dry goods store across the street
still open while she waited on the porch?
And was your hair
wet when you arrived?

She told me you were
at a dance, and I guess
she wasn't smiling.
Is that how you knew?
You asked her what's wrong?
How did you say it? "Mil,
is something wrong?" or
did you say, "What's wrong?"
or, "Aren't you feeling well?"
Well, you said something and she

answered something, "Nothing," or
"It's nothing," or
"What do you mean? Nothing's wrong."
And you said, "Are you sorry we're engaged?"
Did you ask it outright like that really?
She says you did,
but that's someone else.
Then, "No," she said, "just tired," or
"I don't feel so well tonight," or
"I have a headache."
And you kept on dancing,
or went home early,
and, by the next day,
or the next date,
when you saw her,
it was over, the feeling.

II. to my mother

How could you tell your mother, " I
changed my mind. I
don't want to." Silly,
silly girl. What do you mean?
"Mother, Mother I—"
"Just let me stir this soup, Mildred."
"But Mother I wanted to—"
"Hand me the salt. Does this taste like enough to you?
Take a taste."

How could you tell her? How
could you tell anyone?
And so you married the boy who
whistled when he said goodnight,
with one demand: you wouldn't
honeymoon in Atlantic City.
So he bought tickets for
a boat to Florida. A boat to Florida
and a week in Jacksonville.
Lying seasick, neither of you
left the cabin, or maybe
you went to meals and drank some tea,
or raised the cup to your mouth,
then put it down.
In Jacksonville you weren't sick,
just hot, so hot
your fingers swelled like sausages.
You couldn't wear shoes or
your wedding ring. Again
you both lay on the bed, under—
was there a fan? Then
took the train back to Philadelphia.

And afterwards?
Thirty years in the Atlantic City store
thirteen hours a day selling beer.
When you only worked from nine to six
Grandmom would say, "My
you had a short day, Mildred."

Oh, when he asked,
why didn't you say
something, anything, instead of
nothing? But, I saw you
cry when he was sick.

III. to my father

When I call home
you say, "Here's Mother,"
and after we hang up
ask what I said.
But I can remember you
used to sing to me
riding in the car,
"I'd make a string of pearls
out of the dew, for you
for you."

Brother

I used to have a brother and he played with me on our green flowered sofa
and I spent his coin collection on the painted horse in Woolworth's that
    took dimes for rides in a little silver box.
My brother gave me pens and old carbon paper each June when he came home
    from school
and my record player had been his and my typewriter had been his.
The summer I was twelve he took me to Philadelphia. It was hot.
    I wore white pumps and my feet hurt.
I took them off and walked barefoot on the cold tile of the museum and
    my brother smiled at me.
When my brother went to dances he brought me home the favors, a stuffed
    cat or a rubber shrunken head.
He showed me which fingers hit which letters on the keyboard and how to
    swing a tennis racket.
When I was in junior high he told me why french kissing was unacceptable
    for girls my age.
When I was in college he told me why the same was true for making love.

I sat there in that dormitory phone booth while he questioned me and
    questioned me, telling him I didn't know when I was getting married.

Was it in a year?
                No, I don't know.
In five years?
          No.
Then when? In three years?
                Yes, all right, in three years.
                Have it in three years, if that's what you want.
Three years! Three years!
There's only one reason a boy is willing to wait three years.
                Yes. Yes. I confess.

I have a lover.
I've had hundreds of lovers,
     lovers for hours and lovers for years,
     lovers in snatches of rented rooms
     and lovers in deep grasses when the morning sun is dizzy,
     lovers in bus stations smelling of urine and gas fumes,
     lovers in bars where the perfume is heavy and the bass is heavy,
     lovers in Gimbel's double beds, made with wedding present sheets,
     afternoon lovers in unmade beds,
     Saturday night lovers,
     quilted winter lovers with the wind outside,
     new lovers, faithful lovers, married lovers, hurried lovers.

I used to have a brother.
All the books I read were from his shelves.
All my records were stamped with his name.

I had a dream about my father last night

My father sits at the table in the kitchen, reading the Pleasantville Press.
His hair is white and thin, but still wavy, parted in the middle all these
                years.
If I were looking at him, I could see how old he has become.

I remember their wedding picture
(the studio tinted their lips and cheeks pale rose
and the leaves of her white roses are painted a dark forest green),
the only picture not marked with an X,
the only one under glass that day I went through the photograph album
                and the drawers of the breakfront,
X-ing his face, each time it appeared, with a ball-point pen.

I remember when he forbade me to set foot out of my bedroom.
I had to pee. I stood at the doorway crying
until our maid Joe came and picked me up,
carrying me to the toilet,
setting me down, carefully, so my feet wouldn't touch ground,
laughing softly to me, "there baby, we won't let your feet set down."

I cried alot.
Cried when Mrs. Manning in the fifth grade told me I couldn't sing.
Cried when she hollered at the boy who sat next to me.
I cried for Miss America,
for "Father Knows Best."
I loved Robert Young.
He was my father and I was his Betty.
Once, during dinner, I pushed back my chair, ran upstairs, and flung
                myself down on the bed,
waiting for the next step.
This is where Father slowly walks up the stairs,
softly knocks on the door.
"Kitten," he says, and I unlock the door

and he sits by my side on the bed while I sob
and he smoothes back my hair.
But for me there was no soft knocking, no soft "kitten."
My father stormed up the stairs, didn't bother to knock,
simply stood outside the door and said, slowly and loudly, but without
                    yelling,
"Open this door."
I stood there looking up while he looked down.

We moved to Pleasantville when I was almost two.
Every night at dinner I would say, "No like it here. No upstairs.
                    No downstairs. Go home now."
They bought a new dining room set, a light brown table and chairs
                    upholstered in red-orange vinyl.
As they unpacked the chairs, I punched pencil holes in each one.
"Destructive" was the word that Grandmom used.
"You should take this child to a psychiatrist. It's not normal."
I sat behind the sofa cutting my hair.
Mother kept saying, "There's nothing wrong. Everything is fine."
And Father, you said nothing.

In first grade, I learned how to make a "C." That meant "correct."
                    Miss Lee put it on tops of papers that were all correct.
I was so excited, I made C's all over my lined paper and when I got home
                    I made C's up and down the pale green wallpaper in the hall.
Large C's, high and wide as I could reach, great arcs of C's,
          all right, all right, everything is all right.

When you married mother you were looking for two things, you said:
                    a pretty girl and a house with no screaming.
So I cut my hair, and poked holes in the chairs, set fire to the living
                    room rug, drew C's on the wallpaper, and cried.
But not until last night, when I dreamed of you, did I scream.

15

And it would not do to stand over me as you stood over my crib,
ordering, "Stop it. Stop it."
I would not stop.
I'm not your laughing daughter.

Making deep snow prints,
                    hearing the crunch

■

This is the story of Officer Blueberry and me
and my friends and the Lincoln Reservoir
and the rich black muck we walked through
soft gooey muck that slid between our toes on the way to our spot
where we paddled about through the short sea grasses
sliding on our bellies
dipping tongues in to drink the sugared water.
Like lizards, slowly we pulled ourselves up on the beach
and dried in the warm sand
put mud on our asses to keep them from sunburn.
And we were all alone except for some very small animals:
one little worm
maybe half a fingernail long
yellow with an orange dot near the middle of his back
with tiny, very thin legs.
When he sat on the crest of my hand
against the sky
I could see the blue between his legs.
And a second worm
a cream color, the color of my bedroom walls
only more transparent
with a dark brown line down each side of his back.
He climbed stalks of grass and hung on with his sticky back feet,
stuck his neck out, circled, and finding only air
climbed down again.

So we were there
lapping up the water
paddling around
getting to know the little yellow worm
and the cream colored worm with the dark lines
when, in the middle of everything,
we heard a rustle in the blueberry bushes,

and there, right in the middle of the forest,
in the middle of the wilds of the de Cordova Museum.
popped the head of Officer Blueberry
whose mission it was to arrest us
to escort us to the Lincoln District Court
to bring us in front of the judge
charged with swimming naked in the people's drinking water.

But Officer Blueberry just stood there
telling us we didn't look wet to him,
that the Chief was in a bad mood
but we didn't look wet to him.
Oh yes, I said, I do understand. I do.
And as he told us how dry we looked
he took our names and addresses
and our dates of birth including the year
and he wrote it all down on his clipboard.

Meanwhile, we gathered up our shorts and our shirts.
I stuffed three books of matches
a Budweiser can
and a pair of shredded jockey shorts
in my pockets.
Larry asked him if he came through our muck, too.
But no, Officer Blueberry didn't come through our muck.
He wouldn't even let us go back through our muck.
He made us climb through the brambles instead.

Poor watery-eyed officer of a blueberry
defending the reservoir from the likes of us:
Seven naked natives.
How could you move us?
How could you get it across?
You don't look wet to me.

Of course, I understand, I understand.
It's okay, Officer Blueberry.
You don't need to be afraid.
We'll go quietly.
We're not really restless.
Only, you got it all wrong.
Those people who called in weren't complaining.
They were only telling you we had no food.
It was a rescue call.
And you forgot the flask.
No wonder you didn't know what to do.
You were the ice cream man without your white jacket.
We'd like some eskimo pies
an orange ice
and a couple of fudgsicles, please.
Oh, Officer Blueberry we are hungry.
Seven naked natives
all hungry
and there you were with only your shiny badge to protect you.
Nothing to offer to show your good will.
No language in which to tell us,
"Friend. No eat friend."

So you stood
your blue eyes watery as the reservoir
looking so helpless, I wanted to say
take off your blueberry shirt, come down to our sand.
But you misunderstood.
What will they do when they see I have no popsicles
not even a sno-cone in my pocket?
Did you flash on the headlines:
Officer Blueberry Found Missing.

21

Of course,
seven naked people,
no food all day.
Not me, not Officer Blueberry.
I won't take off my shirt.
I know what you're up to.
Oh frightened Officer Blueberry,
we wouldn't eat you.
All I wanted was for you to come down here on the sand
where you could stop impersonating that blueberry
and grow brown in the sun
with us
brown as a berry.

■

Carrying the wood through the deep snow,
dragging back a whole dead branch
trailing behind me like a train
and twigs, bunched in my other hand,
each time I passed
(on the left going and the right coming)
the yellow pee stain in the snow.

September 7

Oh Beverly, do you remember
how we sat together in that brook, touching
our own bodies, wishing
we weren't wearing navy shorts, wishing
we could wear
only our own skin
like the silver birches
like the pebbles in the brook.

I was a pebble in that brook
a pebble with a pink band, and you
in your own skin
under those regulation campers' shorts
were a freckled pear.

The brook soaked through our shorts
and it should have been cold
it should have been too cold for two young girls
to put their bottoms in.

It should have been too cold
we should have gone back
back to change our wet shorts
and dry our private, barely hairy,
parts in towels that mother sewed our names in.

But we didn't.
We sat there where we were
not cold at all

singing softly madrigals

              ride a cock horse
              to banbury cross
              to see a fine lady
              ride on a white horse
              ride on a white cock
              ride on a fine lady
              ride on, ride on

Singing madrigals and touching
bark and leaves and grass that grew beside the brook
wishing we were green and silver like the birch
green and brown like the dirt.

I put my head into a wide crack in the bank
and felt the coolness, dampness
of the earth against my cheeks
against my nose
smelled its dampness.

Like my opening
cool and damp
like the hole in the bank
grass growing around it
brown earthy hole and green grass.

We touched the earth
crumbled it in our hands
dug our fingers in the grass of the bank
caressed the silver bark of the birch
the dry pebbles in the sun
and the cold wet pebbles in the stream
held the pebbles in our hands
and ate the freckled pears.

On Tuesday

I couldn't make love upside down on Tuesday.
The room was very dark,
but I had to see your face.
I cried on Tuesday.
I was thin as tea,
nerve-tender,
as you came to me, quietly
and slowly as dusk.

Celia

Celia, Celia, your name is like cilia,
fine hairs of a paramecium, flapping gently in unison
like a sunny day crew, cilia,
flapping gently like the arms of twenty ballerinas,
cilia, like a flock of gulls,
cilia, fine hair, like the down of your shoulder,
cilia, thick black hair of your lashes,
long fringe of your eyes, dark eyes of Arab women,
all that shows, all that shines, from the chaderi,
cilia, mane, black and wild, mad hair, crazy hair,
electric hair that shimmies like castanets.

Celia, as we smoke I feel the network of my veins,
spider web of capillaries carrying
hot rain mist, thick blood mist,
and the bones of my cheeks pulse
and the bones of my shoulders pulse.
I observe. I observe the fine curly thread snagged in my thumbnail,
delicate, fanned cirrus,
feathery arm of a white barnacle;
the smoke, rising, spiraling, transparent smoke twirling like these letters,
scribbles, lines that double back and swirl into words,
black wet lines, deep trails, like snakes through mud, winding,
flamenco lines that pulse like Celia's hair,
like my hair
that moistens, thick kinky hair,
hair that blows like sand across the desert,
blows like lean seaweed,
dense pelt of hair that
shields my quick life, stiff as a thumb,
straining to lie with you,
my lovelock to yours,
the throb of cilia with cilia.

■

I washed, one by one,
each item of the Salvation Army wardrobe:
dark suit, tie, fedora hat,
sloshing even the perforated shoes and laces
in the green plastic basin.

When they hit water
all the smell came out, sour
like teeth forgotten
in a glass of water by the bed.

What was I doing with this man's clothes?
rinsing out the sweat of June funerals
and high school graduations,
years of Sunday mornings,
train rides, his own wedding?

Who is he? And who am I
to wash his costume here
like breakfast plates?

But I am unquestioning,
accepting my vocation
to wash his clothes,
preparing them
to lie in state, like china
on my kitchen shelf.

Changes

I've stopped using deodorant
and am always bending my head
to smell myself.
I like the smell.
It is new, though,
and I keep checking.

In Celebration

Last night I licked
your love, you love,
like a cat. And
I watched you rise like
bread baking, like
a helium balloon, rise
with the skill of a soufflé,
your love, waving like
passengers on a boat coming in.
My cheek resting on your belly,
moist like a bathroom mirror, resting
in your hair like
dew grass, I drew
your love out like
the head of a turtle, like
an accordion, like
an expandable drinking glass.
I licked
you love, your love,
hard as a lollipop, plump
and tender as a plum.
I held you
like a mitten, like a cup,
and, like the crowds in the spray of a Yellowstone geyser,
like kids splashing in a July fire hydrant,
like a dinner guest biting in a whole tomato,
I gasped,
I laughed,
I feasted on your vintage.

■

It's getting dark outside, and across the street
two men are sitting on the third floor balcony,
after moving in furniture all day,
eating something that I can't make out
something from a white paper napkin,
maybe a watermelon.

Two young men, bending over their watermelon,
eating it in the cool air,
after moving furniture into the house all day.
They wipe their mouths with white napkins
and hold their chins over their hands.

It's getting dark, quickly, and they are silhouettes,
outlines of young men
sitting on the third floor balcony of the house across the street,
eating something, it is impossible to tell what in the darkness,
but bending over as they eat.

Partly to my cat

Walking, I heard the water dripping, running in the gutter
and I didn't walk on.
I stopped, standing in that snow,
        listening to that water,
        watching it through the grating of the gutter,
        watching the grating,
        and listening.
Later, I made dinner, cutting the ends from the string beans slowly,
            feeling the knife crunch neatly through the bean,
            slide across the wooden board.
And I was not so slow as it might seem.
Only, I did not hurry.
I took the garbage out, stepping through the snow,
        snow like string beans,
        crunching under my feet.

The next day I made a tuna fish sandwich,
not listening to the celery,
and the Prudential Center doorman wouldn't let me use his bathroom.
Oh when will I pee, quietly, smiling, on his red carpet?
I don't need a bathroom.
It can happen anywhere at all, like a sneeze.
But we are tied up with ribbons.
We live inside gift-wrapped packages,
        gummed with Christmas seals
        and tagged with the name of our donor,
        rustling about in the colored tissue paper,
        shredding it with our teeth,
        making our nest of scraps.
We live inside briefcases,
    chew the glue from the back of scotch tape,
    lick ink from the navy blue signatures:
We are buckled in top-grade cowhide,

smelling the warmth of the cow,
                    the grass,
                    the slightly soured milk.

Even with sandalwood incense burning at noon
            and oranges preserved in nutmeg and cloves,
even with apples smuggled in sweaters
with the fire from the old kitchen chairs
and the penny-eyed cat showing us how to sit on refrigerators,
we do not always hear.

We must stop:
                    stop eating dinner in the Star Market
                        and making love in subways
                    stop doing isometric exercises on the telephone
                    stop brushing our teeth at red lights.
This can't go on.

Cat: you are the animal that we forget to be.
Your stomach is your suitcase,
while I have 3 bathrobes and
            8 prs. of shoes,
            a checking account,
            5 credit cards,
            and a AAA membership.
This breakfront staggers me.
I cannot carry the bookcases and drapes,
            the rugs, the linens, the dining room table.
This is no gear for a hike, for a life.
How can I leap to the heights of refrigerators weighted like this?

I will unload my relatives and toaster,
            my plumbing, my elevator, my degrees.

I will wash myself, slowly and completely, with my tongue.
I will run,
       like you cat,
              making deep snow prints,
                     hearing the crunch.

Japanese Notebooks
       for Louis

This takes place in Japan. Louis is a man I love in Massachusetts. Beverly, a girlhood friend, living in Japan; Nathan, her husband; Joshua, their child. Zazen is meditation. Sesshin is three days of meditation. These poems are the beginning of an exploration into seven weeks of my life.

■

I have a seat down by the river
in the afternoon and river grass,
bottle caps, bits of glass, sun tinsel on the water.
In the wind tall bamboo poles sway,
boats shift, ropes hang drying in the sun,
the smell is Atlantic City after a storm.

I am here.
I got here, this somewhere, by myself. I,
who cannot find Cohasset, Mass. after driving every Thursday,
have somehow found Matsushima, Pine Tree Island,
this spot by a river.

I thought of asking at the ticket counter.
I'd memorized the question: can you tell me where?
But I saw the bridge and a yellow sweater boy
I followed instead.
After coaching basketball he'll take me to his family.

I am somewhere, called here.
It is a place to be.
If there were no yellow sweater,
no certain miso soup and seersucker yukata after the bath,
would the sun be like this on my face?
Would I hear the same sound of tinny bicycle spokes
and rattling paper that wraps my four orange lillies?
or is there still a girl who lies awake
planning how to get her suitcase to the station,
rewording inquiries?

Thin oyster shells, flaky pastries,
are piled high and down the river
where men in rubber boots bend over.

Ferry Dream. Imagine:

You're travelling here in Japan
and order sliced beef and canned peas in a cafeteria,
but when you return to your table,
Beverly's sitting in your seat, reading a newspaper.

So you pull up another chair.
It's hot; you're sweating.
You unbutton your white blouse,
forgetting you have nothing underneath,
and turn around to take it off.

There you are
facing a crowd of men.
You're scared;
you start explaining you forgot,
but they stand in a semi-circle;
they wanna fuck.

You look each one in the eye
asking him please
listen for a minute.
The leader is large warm flesh.
He says a minute's a long time and feels up your crotch.

Other guys wander in.
One offers you a j. Some are snorting smack.
The leader don't want any.
He wants ta fuck.
You say, "Right. But let's see what they're doing.
If we feel like some now, we can always fuck later."
You go up the stairs to the roof,
to a garden where everyone's nodding.

You look out at the bay:
houses or flowers
all rise up from the shore,
up a mountain; everything
is pale and pastel colors, pink shimmering.
It doesn't matter what danger you're in,
who's there, nothing.

As you watch, you hear the ferry music,
realize, almost, that you're dreaming.
You think, if you could ever really
see such a vision . . .
and as you're thinking, you realize you are.

As the houses come into focus and the lines sharpen,
the colors get darker, the houses get firmer:
it's the back road in Ventnor
where they've filled in the bay.

In your dreaming you sob
and it wakes you
and the ferry is pulling into Hakodate.

■

Yesterday on the ferry I discovered tomato.
Biting into a whole tomato, a small bite, not too deeply,
doing this over a good-sized area,
you too will discover tomato:
in between the firm dividers, wet and slippery as August sex,
        shining blood and pearls.

■

Dear Dad,

Yesterday on the train I sat across from an old man
drinking sake from a half-pint bottle.
Every now and then
he'd cough, pour a little sake, and shift position.
Once I started to open the window,
but he said no.

After an hour or so, he pushed a Pepsi toward me.
Then I offered him a third of my orange.
He ate two sections, squirting himself,
and re-folded his handkerchief
(Do you remember when we used to sit
in the swivel chair in Pleasantville
and you'd say "handkerfish"?).
Later he bought another sake
and an iced coffee for me.
He didn't speak, but when I changed positions,
he made room for my feet.
At first I wondered if he was trying to make up
for having his own way about the window,
but it was more than that.
The crabby old man liked me.

When we got to Matsushima
I gathered up my raincoat and knapsack,
knocking over the empty bottles,
saying "excuse me" and "thank you" and "good-bye."
He kept snapping "hurry up, hurry up."
When I got off I was crying.
That old man pushing sodas was you.

As I'm writing this, a boy asks
"Are you writing a love letter?"
"No," I say, "I'm writing to my father."
Then I say, "Yes."

Bath Dream

I.

Beverly and I go to our apartment
to take a bath together,
but there's a little girl visiting us,
so I take one myself.

II.

I throw out the seaweed
from the water,
then think maybe
I should have saved it to eat.

■

Chuken Hachiko, stone dog statue
still waiting for your master to return
all these years and no one's told you.
Faithful, like the Biltmore clock or Swan & Edgar's,
you've become the rendezvous, waiting place—
Meet'cha at the dog.

Train: Tokyo to Nikko

I.

Neat rows of tender sprouts up through the watery mud;
small square plots, bushy with yellow wheat;
patches of lettuce, 3 heads wide; pom-pom topped onions.
Men and women work bent over.
Their straw hats are
big Pucci flowers among the vegetables.

II.

Brigid peels us an orange
with long red fingernails.
One nail is discolored,
black shows through the polish.
I eat my piece of orange.
It is sour and juicy.
I chew up a seed.

Elevator ride

Going down to the base of the waterfall
this whole carload of yellow-capped children
bounce up and down like daffodils,
squeaking as the numbers light up.

On the way back, my car has no children,
just the creaking of an old man's shoes.

Train: Nikko to Sendai

Old man with your bottle of yellow water
spitting in your newspaper,
chewing on your rice ball.
Are you taking urine to a special doctor?
Are you drinking sake?
Is it smelly? Is it hot?

You show me snapshots from Hollywood and Rome
and Leningrad Park where you pose with someone's bride
(it takes you a long time to fit them back in the envelope),
then put your arm around me to get our picture taken.

At the Fukushima station, I watch you on the platform
walk by the row of plastic bottles
filled with o cha, pale green tea.

Gold tooth Kyushu Doctor,
ask me to go with you,
take me to the hot springs,
take me to the specialists,
take me to the boardwalk where your cousin sits to watch the crowds,
don't just take my picture and go.

Kabuki Theatre

I.

In the lobby was a painting of a crane
in shades of white and gray
except the eye was orange
and the long thin legs were pink.

II.

When we ate custard at the intermission
Susie said she'd pay for mine,
but I said no.
"Don't you ever get lonely?" she said.

■

I wear my hair tied back.
It's not so attractive, but I'm less conspicuous.
How long can I go on, afraid to be seen?

Yes, I am a foreigner—Gaigin—and I am tall and I dress in purple and green.
I have a big head of frizzy hair, hairy legs, and big breasts.
You will not mistake me for a tree.
You will not mistake me for a lamp post
or even a Japanese.

When your school children stare, I'll stick out my tongue.
When your men whistle, I'll unbutton my blouse.
When you ask for my autograph, I'll write Greta Garbo.

I'll eat with chopsticks, but if you look too long
I'll drop my face and lick like a cat.
I'll wear a bathing suit in the public baths and go naked in the stores.
I'll go barefoot rather than leave my shoes in the foyer.
I'll wear high-heels and look over the tops of your heads.

If you ask me again, can I use a Japanese toilet, I'll shit in the bushes.
If you won't give me toilet paper, I'll drip dry in the streets.
You needn't explain your Japanese beds,
I'll sleep standing on one leg like a flamingo.

I will talk in Hebrew and Iroquois
and for writing I'll use hieroglyphics or Morse Code or Braille.
I'll knit a long trail of angora wool from my hotel to the park
          so I need never ask directions.
I will pretend I'm a deaf mute.

You will not mistake me.

Not even at Tokyo Station or at the Waseda Baseball Game
will I go unnoticed.
I'll stare at you from the ads on the train,
                from your snapshots of Mt. Fuji,
                from the gold leaf buddhas.
You will see my face in the railroad man,
                in the farmer planting rice,
                in the dance hall hostess.

When you ask what America is like, I'll say,
        America is very nice and very wonderful.
When you ask if I like Japan,
        Japan is very nice and very wonderful.
Am I a student?

Yes. Yes, I'm a student.
My eyes are microscopes.
My skin, a sliver-thin galvanometer.
I am litmus paper, calipers, gage.
Tweezer-fingered, I hold your goods to the light.

I study the texture of your hair; your combs with teeth so fine
they are the underside of mushrooms.
I study the orange eye of your crane,
your origami crab's accordion legs,
the pattern of the leaves that have fallen into the water.
I study three plastic bottles on a ledge,
each with a different amount of tea left,
and a small tea bag, resting on the bottom like a fish.

I'll be wearing yellow socks, Italian driving shoes from L. L. Bean,
        and my mother's signet ring: MW–1927.
Please say hello when you see me.

Fish Dream

Celia skins small live fish,
splits them in half,
opening each side.
Then with thumb and finger she pinches the heart,
a dark purple-brown umeboshi plum.

I do one too,
press my fingers, pop the sac
(like a little balloon ball
sucked into the mouth).

When a woman tries to talk to me
I say, "leave me alone,
I've just been killing fish."

■

To explain how
waiting for the pleasure boat,
looking out at the Tokugawa River
      and the old grounded boats,
holding a slim can of orange juice,
I could let
go, just
let the can drop.

At the baseball game

Streamers arc the sky like fish line
catching sun, then wave down.

Everyone throws bits of newspaper and streamers.
Everyone twirls red and white parasols.
Shuji Saito asks if I want one.
No, I like the sun.
But, for a remembrance?
No, not really.
After the game he buys me one.

Streamers catch in trees,
wave, like kite tails, in the wind.

53

Beverly and I take a four-day trip

Nathan broke his ankle an hour after we left;
Beverly's cough got worse, developed into chills and fever.
They sent distress signals to each other:
      I'm sick.
      You can't desert me now.
      And what about the child?

I had ridden off with Bev,
separating them:
      He, on his large mat,
      she, in the twin bed across from mine.

The next night they were back together in Akiya.
And I was in a hostel in Kurashiki
throwing up in a row of toilets.

For Louis

I know you. You're a great sperm whale.
You're Polaris. You're a giant stack of pancakes.
You think I've lost track of you.
You think I don't know what you're up to.
Ten thousand miles and an ocean and a desert away.
But the Big Dipper shines in the sky here too.
There's McDonald's at Shinjuku Station
and the radio plays, "like the flowers need the rain,
you know I need you."

I know where you are.
I see you in my brown velvet chair,
the blue cow parked in your driveway,
all my boxes in the basement.

When I stand in the garden, washing my face,
mist rising from the bay,
I see you in the basin, in that morning canoe
we got for free. The fisherwoman laughing,
"I hope I never get so old
I can't remember being young."

I see you on your bicycle. I see you making bean soup.
I see you our first day together, walking with the dogs.
In my big rubber boots, I stop
and watch you coming toward me.
You're Ichabod Crane and country and smiling
and I think how it would be to see you walking toward me
years from now. I think what it would be to love you.

I want you to see it all:
the woman who stops to get a drink, spreading her feet like a giraffe in Kenya,

the whale gills like huge false eyelashes,
the Smo players throwing salt,
the vermilion snake bridge,
the spider webs, misting trees like Spanish moss,
        big raindrops, suspended, shining like fish in nets,
the blue birds flying on shopping bags,
the fat jelly fish kites,
the scenes from the life of the Emperor Meiji:
        "Empress sending a poetic epistle
            to the Emperor traveling in the north-east provinces."

I think of you in the north-east provinces,
eating bagels and lox in the car,
my finger freezing from spreading the cream cheese.

Lou, think of August, where can we meet?
England, Ralph's cabin?
Nepal? Would you like?
Oh, I wish you had a map
so you could see where I am.

Lemon

Sliced flat of lemon, wet and shining,
sliced fruit of lemon, wet in its own juices,
beading in its lemon juice,
sliced through open sections,
flat lemon.

■

Barbara came to Japan with her husband Bill and their child, Lance, to learn macrobiotic cooking. Two years later, she's waiting for a ticket home to Minnesota.

In between she gave birth to two babies. Bill read several books before the first and insisted he knew how. But the baby died. Now, the children have bronchitis; she has asthma; Bill studies Akido and says her cooking's still not right.

When Beverly and I arrive with a watermelon and a yellow gladiola, Barbara hands the flower back, saying, "You arrange it. You're good at that."

I'm sick of all you Japanese women,
    obeying your husbands,
    indulging your sons.
    You're a lousy example.
I'm sick of all you American women,
    trying to be like them,
    feminine and yin.
    You're making a mistake.
Macrobiotics, you're a no-good teacher.
Women, do you know
what the qualities of yin really are?

Japan's a nice place and all that,
but it's not for us.
You're an oaf if you laugh open-mouth.
You're a dyke if you take big steps.
You're a very bad girl, if you're not Japanese.

Go home Barbara,
leave the raw fish and the Tokyo smog,
the hot water heater that's not paid off,
your husband, his Akido, astrology, and acupuncture.

Go back to Minnesota and toast an English muffin,
drive a cab, eat in restaurants,
do the turkey trot;
dig for sand crabs with your babies,
kiss your mother, run for mayor.

You arrange it.

■

At the top of the hill
the shrine is not blue and red and green.
There are no gold-tongued dragons,
        fat-toothed and rose-nippled,
no warrior gods,
        no God of Wind squeezes his white snake sack,
        or red God of Thunder beats his halo of drum heads.

No Shinto priestesses dance in red and white loose robes
        with golden bells or silver swords
        or sashes flowing from their sleeves.

There are no Virginians, no French, no Japanese
        school children in green caps
        and plastic raincoats with sleeves too long.

There are no old men blowing bird whistles,
no soba stands with noodles dripping through the trays;
no ticket sellers, ticket takers, postcards, shopping bags, mausoleums,
        cubicles for storing shoes.

Here, is the wooden shrine, unpainted,
                                straw sandals
                                tied to the door.
Here, through the slats, is
        barely in the dark
        the large seated figure
        on a chair, an Eastern Moses.

The sounds are of the birds calling out
and water flowing and churning in the power house,
leaves moving in the wind,
or some small animal who shifts in the grass.

Moving

Cucumber and muenster cheese slices on the way to Akiya,
Beverly in a white sun hat with pink flowers.
I'm in the back of the truck with the boxes.

At the summer house

Beverly coughs softly. She is wearing a blue and white dotted sleep dress and sews on a rope basket, stitching slowly and evenly. I can hear her thread pulling through the rope. I look up at her, but I don't look too long or she'll notice me watching.

An ant walks quickly across the straw rug. Outside it is dark. There are only the two street lights down the road. And the sound of frogs and crickets. Beverly finishes her sewing for tonight and gets up. I ask about her cough. She says it's just getting Tokyo out of her system.

She goes to her room and carries Joshua out to the bathroom in his white underwear, talking to him softly, sitting him on the seat. "Dozo," please, she says. Then she carries him back and he is asleep. It is probably around 10. Beverly flushes the toilet. As it refills it makes a sound like a foghorn. When it stops, the frogs and the crickets are clear again.

We were the girls who dressed in velvet skirts
        and hitched to Tanglewood, high heels stuffed in our purses;
we wrote stories about little girls with elephant trunk toes;
and we never wore underpants, not even on the subway.

Here, I am a guest in your house.

All the times you reversed the charges, wore my clothes,
arrived at midnight with a large straw hat and the Sunday Times,
no luggage, no money, no return trip ticket.

Now, you tell me to dress for breakfast.

You show me how the trains work,
take me grocery shopping,
and I'm on my own.
You won't even let me come along to climb Mt. Fuji.

Only once do you tell me about yourself,
your marriage, that you're
committed to Nathan, but
every spring you fall in love.

Oh why then, Bev,
don't you fall in love with me?

■

When I left the temple
last night's rain hung on the ends of pine needles,
sat flat on the leaves of the ichi tree like transparent silver beetles.
The onions in the field smelled strong,
the mud was squishy,
my knees were weak.

Then I saw a large snail, about the length of my thumb,
crawling along, antennae waving slowly in front of him.
God he was slow
and a little gravelly (it must be very irritating when he pulls inside).
There was also a minute white bug, running around on him, very fast.

■

Everywhere, a botanical garden is the same.
Latin names in Roman letters:
rosa rugusa, nicotiana tabacum, asparagus officianalis.
Science, I never thought to love you.

Learning all the phylum, genus, species
in tenth grade biology—
why not call an elm an elm. We all know
what we mean. It never sank in
Japanese don't say elm.

Here, I am in my world again.
I have the words. I have the names.
I can know the thing in its name.
Use a word three times and it's yours.

Flaming orange flowers, dark purple centers,
        are *papaver orientale.*
A little gray green plant, close to the ground, leaves shaped like roses
        is *sedum cauticelum.*
And in between *urtica platyphylla* and *chloranthus japonicus,*
I can see the empty space
where *cannabis sativa* used to be.

This garden's mine.
I know lilacs lead to the toilet
and Way Out is by the peonies,
pink and purple heads thrown back.

I am at home here in the herbacious plant garden.
I fill my notebook with the names of things.
The marsh and valley forest,

the Queen Anne's lace, and I,
we belong to each other.
I even pick, illegally, little blue and yellow flowers.

Then, at closing, I leave,
passing in front of a government building,
deep pansies, thick brown and orange velvet,
blue-purple velvet, maroon velvet, white,
without any signs.

■

One more dream about returning home and a neutral meeting with Louis. Didn't bother to write it down. Just put some repellent on my face and feet and went back to sleep.

Neutral Feeling: I'm the neutral feeling, colorless and odorless as oxygen or
                 ozone.
                 I have no form. I take up no room.
                 I live in the stomach when it's empty,
                 between corrugated dividers,
                 between your arm and your side
                 when your hand is resting on your hip.
                 I am routine.
                 There is little to say about me.

Excitement: I am excitement.
                 I race through the Nairobi airport—
                 yellow chalk, yellow health cards, the smell of his yellow hair.
                 I ride the waves in the Long Island ocean
                 when they're ten-feet high and you shoot from the crest,
                 crash around, come up laughing, strap broken, and wild.
                 Be like me.
                 I'm a samurai.
                 I say "fuck you" my first time on TV.

Neutral Feeling: I know very well who you are.
                 And I know what I look like next to you.
                 But I'm necessary. You'll see.
                 I am the measure, the ruler, the line
                 between yes and no,
                         sweet and sour,
                         hot and cold.
                         in and out.

I am the middle of every maxim: fish nor fowl,
                                hide nor hair,
                                yin nor yang.
I am neither the snow at the top of Mt. Fuji,
        nor the red dirt at the base of the Grand Canyon.
I am not the cedars, nor am I the mosses.
Nothing you can name,
nothing you can describe with your poet's names and images
   am I.
Beyond those sensations, neutral, past caring—
but I get off the subject.
I get carried away.
With you I'm seduced into crazy talk.
Who can live at your pitch? Who has the strength?
It's too hard for me.
I am relief.

I was born in Philadelphia, raised in New Jersey
on top of the Hy-Grade Wines and Liquors store.
I didn't grow up in Egyptian deserts,
wasn't fed on persimmon,
                wrapped in sharkskin,
                given baby ocelots for Easter.
What do you expect?
What do you want from me?

Excitement: Christopher Columbus! Streets paved with gold!
               India, spices, silks, gunpowder.
               I'm a fifth-grade explorer off to new worlds.

               Oh Lou, come with me, this is the life.
               Live with the Zulus, fish through the ice,

marry a Viking, drink blood, grow scales.
Please don't be ordinary.
Don't make me be ordinary.
Help me stop being ordinary.
I want to speed through an eclipse like a bat.

On my way to pick up mended sandals
I pass a lady, old as burdock root,
a face of wrinkled silk.

Sweat moons under my arms,
thin dark-purple crescents
under my breasts,

walking late
in the afternoon of a hot day
to the shoemaker.

Beverly speaks

I don't know what she expected of me. Really we were glad to have her. She wasn't in the way, but all the time there was this tension about her. Her voice was so high, I was never sure if she was going to laugh or cry. And so hurried, always rushing somewhere. No sooner had she got here than she was off to Hokkaido. Hadn't been here more than a week, and not a word from her the whole time she was away. Not a postcard. She goes off, doesn't know a soul, can't speak the language, and oh, did I worry. And didn't even call on her birthday. That is, it wasn't her birthday, but I'd gotten the dates mixed up. I thought her birthday was on the 6th instead of the 16th. And Nathan and I both thought, she'll surely give us a call on her birthday.

And her crying. Like the time she invited that man to dinner. It was the day before the party (I'd planned this party to introduce her to everyone). And I was cleaning the house, getting ready. She's on the phone with this man and just invites him for dinner. Doesn't ask me, or anything. I tell her it's really not convenient, when there's so much to do. And I'd have to make something special. But she gets upset and starts to cry. I tell her, look at it from my point of view, but it makes it hard to say anything when she's always breaking down like that. Crying to me is something you do when something's really wrong. Sure you cry for joy too. . . . I was going to take her to the herbal doctor, get her something for the crying, but I didn't have time.

When she comes back from Hokkaido, we're in the process of moving to the summer house, you know, packing and boxes all over, and we have to clear everything out and put it in storage. But I promised her we'd go to Kyoto for a few days. I could use a vacation too, hadn't been away from Joshua one night since he was born. I was going to leave him with Nathan and we'd go off for a few days together, go to the shrine sales, maybe to Kabuki, visit oji-san and oba-san. Then I'd return and she could go on farther South. But the night before I got this horrible cold and I felt terrible leaving Nathan with all the moving, and with Joshua too. He told me I ought to stay home, but I didn't want to let her down. So the next morning we got on the train and met Morris and

Brigid in Kyoto. It was so good to see them. We had lunch at this wonderful tempura place. Morris and Brigid have so little money. They ordered one meal and split it between them. So I ordered another and made them eat most of it. The next morning we went to the sauna. By the time I got out, I felt so bad I just had to leave. I called Nathan to meet me and got on the first train to Tokyo. Well, when I got to the station, Satoko was there instead of Nathan. He broke his foot an hour after we left and was home in a cast. I knew I should never have gone.

She stayed down in Kyoto for another week or so and then one night when we'd been out to dinner, we returned to the summer place and she was sitting there in the kitchen eating a bowl of rice. She wasn't supposed to return for two or three more weeks, since Morris and Brigid were staying with us and it was such a small house. And she says, just like that, she's going home. I couldn't believe it. She had hardly gotten here. And the next month, in August, we were going to spend time together, maybe work on an astrology book for children.

Well, the day before she leaves, I'm going to the beach and I ask her if she wants to come along. We go down there together, spread out newspapers on the sand, lie down. And I ask her, "What's happening?" I don't remember the whole conversation, but she says she felt out of place, she wanted to fit in. I tell her she had a place. She was here. She took up space. But I don't think she heard me. She said she was lonely. But, there was nothing to be afraid of. I tried to explain how it's like traffic on a highway. Nathan and Joshua and I are the main stream of traffic and she comes in off a ramp. She has to go the speed of the traffic.

It's true. I didn't have much time for her, but she was on vacation and my life kept on going. I couldn't just take off and play the whole day. I was sorry I couldn't take her around and show her everything. But I just didn't have the time. I thought I explained that before she came. I really don't know what she expected from me.

Last night in the baths

When I turned on my spigot, no water came out
so the old woman motioned me to share hers.
She was hunchbacked, her breasts were only nipples.

I moved closer, embarrassed
at my straight spine and full breasts.
I wanted to wash her back
but was afraid to ask.

When she rose, she looked hairless,
loose smooth arm pits and sex,
but I couldn't see well—she was bent over,
and held her hands
like a Botticelli Venus.

The night before sesshin

The frog croaks. Mosquitoes buzz around.
I'm a little hungry.
Today I ate a bowl of rice,
                    miso soup,
                    3 sweets at tea class,
                    and half an orange.

What are these women doing here with their face cream at sesshin?
One brushes her hair with a thin cloth over the bristles.

        Not even my voice goes out from me,
        my eyes don't penetrate anyone.
        To say: I am a part of wherever I am,
        this scene would be different without me—
        I believe it.

                                "There's nothing to be scared of.
                                Only your legs will hurt and
                                    you'll be bored."

Why am I sitting sesshin?
to experience it,
to accept pain,
to rise above circumstances,
to have something to do.

                                "From the moment we're born
                                we're a thorn in the world's side."

There's a toilet near the women's sleeping room,
but it's for the head monk, so we should use it only if it rains.
We can fill our rice bowl and soup bowl twice, and the little bowl is for pickles.
Tea is poured into the rice bowl,
then we clean the bowls by rubbing a pickle over them.

> "You will experience what it means
> to have the bottom fall out of
> your own thoughts about
> persevering and suffering."

I'm preparing to walk in space, sit on a flagpole, live underwater.
It's never been done before.

Sesshin—the word has become my mantra,
the word has become a pass word, a passage.
California, at the gold rush.

> "You get so stoned out on sesshin,
> the pain doesn't matter."

I'll be part of a group
We'll drink tea at the end
and laugh at the pain in our knees.

Through that endurance, I'll be accepted.
Through that endurance, I'll accept,
stop struggling with my loneliness,
stop thinking Boston will save me,
stop thinking sesshin will save me.

"It is impossible to look directly with your own eyes at the raw reality of your own face. Because zazen actualizes the reality of the life of the self, there is no reason to think you will perceive it."

Sesshin

The first day of sesshin. I wake up to four bongs, quick put on clothes, pee, change my tampax which doesn't need it, and run to the zendo. I enter, bow, turn and bow, then sit in the half lotus and try to keep thoughts from sticking in my mind. After the first half hour, sitting is difficult. I wonder how I'll get through the day, let alone three days. The man next to me keeps drifting to the side, then jerking upright. Two bells: I bow, rise, bow once more, turn and bow, and then kinhin (walking zazen). Back to our cushions and begin again.

When the bell rings this time we run to the dining room, get our bowls and kneel at the table. First I try to sit at the wrong end where the monks are. I'm so slow there are no places left. Someone fills my rice bowl with very hot cereal and the seaweed is passed. I'm blowing on my cereal, inhaling air, trying to get it down. I've only just begun when everyone else is finished. The tea's already coming. The bucket comes, and still I'm eating, holding up the works. After that we have a half hour to relax and wash. I drink some hot water, hoping to shit and stand in the yard a few minutes. Steam rises from my cup. It's 6:30.

Back to the zendo. The next five hours are sitting broken by kinhin. I'm still hopeful. I've been able to maintain the half lotus position. The shadow of the wood panel gets smaller and disappears. The grain is like the grove of bamboo trees in the temple yard. Already it's getting hot. I am still and don't sweat much. I spend little time not clinging to thoughts. The pain moves up to include my hip joints. I wish I'd soon transcend time. I think of my mother in nurses' training, saying God gives you strength for one day at a time. Say to yourself, can I make today? I translate that into breaths and ask, can I take one more? In the middle of a breath I want to move. I know there are more breaths beyond that one. They're out there following too close.

The five hours are done. At lunch the man next to me takes my bowl. I see everyone bringing back soy bean soup, so I pick up our other bowls to get noodles. When I get back to my seat, the man has left me rice. I have noodles, rice, and no soup. Afraid to lose time, I start eating the noodles without soup.

A man across the table notices and smiles. We're not supposed to greet each other, so I look down.

At one we go back to the zendo. This time I'm going to really try not to cling to thoughts. I must live out the reality of my life and that is, right now, zazen. I imagine meeting Louis. I think of the pain and going home. In Japan I want Boston. In Boston I wanted Japan. The day gets very hot. I change positions and know I'm annoying the man on my right. I'm sorry I ever mentioned his wobbling. The pain in my knees and hips is strong. I worry I'll pull something and always have a weak joint. I think about Mom's bad hip. But of course she was a lot older than me and had been swinging that heavy ice-box door for 20 years.

In the 9th hour of sitting, I decide the reality of my life is that I want to go home. I'll stay in Kyoto another week, return to Akiya for a few days, and then to Boston. I resolve to sit the next two days in gratitude. I feel terrific and think the hour must surely be over. It drags on interminably. I can't even begin to keep a half lotus. I can't figure out what I'm doing this for, can't call up anything to keep me going. I squirm and endure.

Supper, without any hitches, rest and the last two hours. I sit in a loose, cross-legged position and put my knees up some of the time. There's a pouring rain and I wish there'd be lightning or a storm so big the temple's washed away.

Second day: This morning, during the first hour of sitting, I realize I don't want to wait two weeks. I sit through the second hour, leave a note, and walk out.

I have my green knapsack. I have my plaid suitcase. I sit on a bench at a bus stop, my legs dangling down. A bus comes, stops, and goes on.

An opened can of mandarin oranges lies in the gutter water, a few orange slices spilled out, wet, clarified.

■

I am tired of being the child, the maiden aunt,
the Poor Miss Bass who never had any chemistry,
back with all those freshmen, too old and unprepared.
I'm tired of sitting through the sports festival
watching the cheerleaders, accurate and graceless,
the girls with fat knees,
the boys straining, lips pulled inward, eyes, small pig-like slits.
I'm tired of saving theatre programs, writing in my diary,
drinking ginger ale, dreaming of underpants slit at the crotch
like the ones in uptown boardwalk windows.

I'm tired of masturbating
and not masturbating,
tired of scaring men away when I stand up or laugh.
My opened palm is a fan of green leaves,
my fingers, brown and glossy, polished wood,
but they are not enough.

After the basketball game, when Takeo and I sit in the back seat,
his shoulder touches mine as we go around a curve:
there is a surge in my cunt, in my lungs, through my bowels.
Then, a second wave of
almost repulsion, telling me how closed I have become.
Like the windows of air conditioned trains,
like cellophane around a candy box,
like the seal of a whiskey bottle or of a letter,
I am insulated.
I am a Catholic school girl.
I am a widowed woman.

An old man blows me kisses on the street.
A child gives me sweet azuki bean cakes.

Then I ride on the bus next to a fraternity boy from Texas.
Like the night we stopped in North Carolina,
I was still half asleep, went into the diner, toward the bathroom.
Some men in a booth just laughing at me, in my hiking boots,
my frizzy hair, my glasses.
I knew I was beautiful, so I just smiled.
But here I don't know it;
there's nothing to remind me.
Only lovely Japanese women, shy and promising,
ready to undo their summer kimono for the Texas boys.

I've had enough of this.
I want Boston
where men don't check their watches
and I can let my nipples show through colored t-shirts.
I want Boston where I scream and yodel,
pay electric bills, drive a car, unlock the door to my apartment.
Boston, where I know my ass
not just for shitting, my legs for more than transportation,
where more than one man wants to fuck and read me stories,
eating yogurt, calling information for the weather in Maine.

I've had it.
Call the airport.
Get the luggage. Wire Western Union.
Give my regards to Broadway.
Draco the Snako is splitting from here.

■

Oh Japan, I won't be here even until the end of the rains.
Your rice plants will grow yellow and brown without me
and I've never climbed Mt. Fuji or seen the inland sea.

Japan, the water blue tiles of your roofs are beautiful,
            the small deep pendant eggplants of your vines are beautiful.
It is here with you I learned to love the rain
                                    and to eat in restaurants alone.

Japan, forgive me for peeing in your public baths,
                for walking out on sesshin,
                for the time I didn't pay on the street car.
Japan, forgive me that I hate your sweet cakes and your nervous clerks.

The first day I was here,
I took a tentative walk down the 7th circle
with all the big trucks
and I tried very hard to think you were a nice place to be.

But it's time for me to go home now.
Even my periods are screwed up.
It's summer and I'm a young woman,
you're a winter-time country.
You wear woolen bands around your middle
and sleep under heavy quilts.

I'll remember Pine Tree Islands, turtle island and whale island,
I'll remember bunches of children holding out autograph books and caramels.

But there's a third floor room in Arlington, Mass.,
an old lavender nightgown, and a sun-burned man.
I'm going to lie awake
and listen to him breathe.

To Beverly, after

"Any act is pure that does not shrink
from its logical conclusions."
                    —Trouffaut

It all becomes clear, clear and simple.
All the images that come are simple images:
water pouring over big round stones,
leaf clusters, their spring green surface clear as kindergarten skin.

I was determined to be mad,
not to be cajoled with a walk around the zoo.
But the rain was rainy, and I love rain.
It was morning, that's my favorite time.
We were walking—and I didn't know why,
but I was enjoying myself.

You ate your pancakes one at a time
and didn't remember owing $50 from our trip to Vermont in '66.
Finally you said, "What do *you* think was wrong?"
        "You were afraid.
          Something about me made you clutch
          onto Nathan and Joshua."
"Let's go to the museum," you said.

Among the Greek statues, you told me,
"I don't know if you ever knew
but at Camp I had an affair with the swimming counsellor.
We used to meet sometimes at night. I'd make up an excuse.
I felt I was cheating on you."

The pieces, red, silver, burnt umber,
all the funny shaped pieces, all the wrong textures,

all those pieces that could never make a quilt,
all those pieces I didn't know were pieces
(magazine glossies before they're clipped,
a rotting shoe form before it's mounted),
pieces lying around in all the wrong mosaics
now gather at morning flag call on the lawn of Blue Mountain Camp.

You told me not to come to breakfast in my nightgown,
not to invite Don Campbell for dinner
("I just can't handle that," you said),
you told me Steve would never make me feel like a woman.
We always got happy when we were alone.

Nathan flirted with me to deny it.
You held your baby between us to deny it.
I ignored my dreams to deny it.
I thought, she doesn't love me.
You thought, what is it she's not telling.
And we all went around saying to ourselves, something's wrong.

We walk through obelisks; we walk through rain.
When you make up the cot in the basement, your mother says,
"You have a big bed. Have Ellen sleep with you."

You and me, Bev, Amelia Erhardt,
and all those other ladies of the poems,
ladies of the night, freckle-faced girls with beaver smiles.
We are lovers. We are loved.
I've come home to my wavy-haired mother,
and skinny Pat, three years older,
8th grade Maris who said one of us should be a boy,
Marcia slipping her hand to my front,
Celia naming Louis the devil between us,

Roz, Paula, Joanne, Sally,
lovely women of my women's group.
There's been a reconciliation, there's been a mend.
Everything I think of makes a different sense.